50 Pie Dishes

By: Kelly Johnson

Table of Contents

- Apple Pie
- Cherry Pie
- Pumpkin Pie
- Pecan Pie
- Blueberry Pie
- Lemon Meringue Pie
- Key Lime Pie
- Banana Cream Pie
- Chocolate Cream Pie
- Sweet Potato Pie
- Peach Pie
- Blackberry Pie
- Strawberry Rhubarb Pie
- Coconut Cream Pie
- Custard Pie
- Lemon Pie
- Mince Pie
- Maple Cream Pie
- Chocolate Silk Pie

- Raspberry Pie
- French Silk Pie
- Buttermilk Pie
- Meringue Pie
- Apple Crumble Pie
- Caramel Apple Pie
- Mixed Berry Pie
- Huckleberry Pie
- S'mores Pie
- Salted Caramel Pie
- Apricot Pie
- Pear Pie
- Almond Joy Pie
- Honey Pie
- Brown Sugar Pie
- Orange Cream Pie
- Kiwi Pie
- Peanut Butter Pie
- Ice Cream Pie
- Chiffon Pie
- Rhubarb Pie

- Pineapple Pie
- Mocha Pie
- Blackberry Custard Pie
- Chocolate Peanut Butter Pie
- Praline Pie
- Banana Foster Pie
- Bourbon Pecan Pie
- Bourbon Sweet Potato Pie
- Grapefruit Pie
- Spiced Pear Pie

Apple Pie

Ingredients:

- 2 1/2 lbs apples (Granny Smith or Honeycrisp), peeled, cored, and sliced
- 1 tbsp lemon juice
- 3/4 cup granulated sugar
- 1/4 cup brown sugar
- 1 tsp cinnamon
- 1/4 tsp nutmeg
- 1 tbsp cornstarch
- 2 tbsp butter, cut into small pieces
- 1 package of pie crusts (or homemade if preferred)

Instructions:

1. Preheat oven to 425°F (220°C).
2. Toss apple slices with lemon juice, sugars, cinnamon, nutmeg, and cornstarch in a large bowl.
3. Roll out one pie crust and place it in a 9-inch pie pan. Fill with the apple mixture and dot with butter.
4. Roll out the second pie crust and place it over the apples. Trim the edges and crimp to seal. Cut slits in the top crust to allow steam to escape.
5. Bake for 45-50 minutes, until crust is golden and filling is bubbling.
6. Let cool before serving.

Cherry Pie

Ingredients:

- 4 cups fresh or frozen cherries
- 1 cup granulated sugar
- 2 tbsp cornstarch
- 1 tbsp lemon juice
- 1/2 tsp almond extract (optional)
- 2 tbsp butter
- 1 package of pie crusts (or homemade if preferred)

Instructions:

1. Preheat oven to 400°F (200°C).
2. In a saucepan, combine cherries, sugar, cornstarch, lemon juice, and almond extract. Cook over medium heat until the mixture thickens and starts to boil. Remove from heat and stir in butter.
3. Roll out one pie crust and place it in a 9-inch pie pan. Pour the cherry mixture into the crust.
4. Roll out the second pie crust and place it over the filling. Trim, seal, and crimp the edges. Cut slits in the top for ventilation.
5. Bake for 40-45 minutes, until the crust is golden and the filling is bubbling.
6. Let cool before serving.

Pumpkin Pie

Ingredients:

- 1 can (15 oz) pumpkin puree
- 3/4 cup granulated sugar
- 1/2 tsp cinnamon
- 1/4 tsp nutmeg
- 1/4 tsp ginger
- 1/4 tsp cloves
- 2 large eggs
- 1 1/2 cups heavy cream
- 1 tsp vanilla extract
- 1 prepared pie crust

Instructions:

1. Preheat oven to 425°F (220°C).
2. In a large bowl, whisk together pumpkin, sugar, spices, eggs, cream, and vanilla extract.
3. Pour the mixture into the prepared pie crust.
4. Bake for 15 minutes, then reduce temperature to 350°F (175°C) and bake for another 40-45 minutes, until the filling is set.
5. Let the pie cool before serving.

Pecan Pie

Ingredients:

- 1 1/2 cups pecan halves
- 3/4 cup corn syrup
- 1/2 cup brown sugar
- 1/4 cup granulated sugar
- 3 large eggs, beaten
- 1 tsp vanilla extract
- 2 tbsp melted butter
- 1/4 tsp salt
- 1 prepared pie crust

Instructions:

1. Preheat oven to 350°F (175°C).
2. In a large bowl, combine corn syrup, brown sugar, granulated sugar, eggs, vanilla, butter, and salt. Mix well.
3. Stir in the pecans.
4. Pour the mixture into the prepared pie crust.
5. Bake for 50-55 minutes, or until the filling is set and golden.
6. Let cool before serving.

Blueberry Pie

Ingredients:

- 4 cups fresh or frozen blueberries
- 1 cup granulated sugar
- 1/4 cup cornstarch
- 1 tbsp lemon juice
- 1 tsp vanilla extract
- 1 tbsp butter
- 1 package of pie crusts (or homemade if preferred)

Instructions:

1. Preheat oven to 375°F (190°C).
2. In a saucepan, combine blueberries, sugar, cornstarch, lemon juice, and vanilla extract. Cook over medium heat, stirring until the mixture thickens and starts to boil.
3. Roll out one pie crust and place it in a 9-inch pie pan. Pour the blueberry mixture into the crust and dot with butter.
4. Roll out the second pie crust and place it over the filling. Trim, seal, and crimp the edges. Cut slits in the top for ventilation.
5. Bake for 45-50 minutes, until the crust is golden and the filling is bubbly.
6. Let cool before serving.

Lemon Meringue Pie

Ingredients:

- 1 prepared pie crust
- 1 1/2 cups water
- 1 cup granulated sugar
- 1/4 cup cornstarch
- 1/4 tsp salt
- 3 large egg yolks, beaten
- 1/2 cup fresh lemon juice
- 2 tbsp lemon zest
- 1 tbsp butter
- 3 large egg whites
- 1/2 tsp cream of tartar
- 6 tbsp granulated sugar

Instructions:

1. Preheat oven to 350°F (175°C).
2. In a saucepan, combine water, sugar, cornstarch, and salt. Cook over medium heat, stirring constantly, until the mixture thickens and comes to a boil.
3. Remove from heat and whisk in the egg yolks, lemon juice, lemon zest, and butter.
4. Pour the lemon filling into the prepared pie crust.
5. In a separate bowl, beat egg whites with cream of tartar until soft peaks form. Gradually add sugar and beat until stiff peaks form.

6. Spread the meringue over the lemon filling, making sure to seal the edges.

7. Bake for 10-12 minutes, until the meringue is golden brown.

8. Let cool before serving.

Key Lime Pie

Ingredients:

- 1 1/2 cups sweetened condensed milk
- 1/2 cup fresh lime juice
- 3 large egg yolks
- 1 prepared graham cracker crust
- 1/4 cup whipped cream (for topping)

Instructions:

1. Preheat oven to 350°F (175°C).
2. In a bowl, whisk together condensed milk, lime juice, and egg yolks until smooth.
3. Pour the filling into the graham cracker crust.
4. Bake for 15 minutes, then remove from the oven and let cool.
5. Refrigerate for at least 4 hours before serving.
6. Top with whipped cream before serving.

Banana Cream Pie

Ingredients:

- 1 prepared pie crust
- 2 cups whole milk
- 1/2 cup granulated sugar
- 1/4 cup cornstarch
- 1/4 tsp salt
- 4 large egg yolks
- 2 tbsp unsalted butter
- 1 tsp vanilla extract
- 2 ripe bananas, sliced
- 1 cup heavy cream (whipped)

Instructions:

1. Preheat oven to 350°F (175°C).
2. In a saucepan, combine milk, sugar, cornstarch, and salt. Cook over medium heat, stirring constantly, until thickened.
3. In a separate bowl, whisk egg yolks and temper with some of the hot milk mixture. Gradually add the egg yolks to the saucepan and cook for 2-3 minutes.
4. Remove from heat and stir in butter and vanilla extract.
5. Pour the custard into the prepared pie crust and let cool.
6. Once cool, top with sliced bananas and whipped cream.
7. Refrigerate for at least 2 hours before serving.

Chocolate Cream Pie

Ingredients:

- 1 prepared pie crust
- 1 1/2 cups whole milk
- 1/2 cup heavy cream
- 3/4 cup granulated sugar
- 1/4 cup cornstarch
- 1/4 tsp salt
- 3 large egg yolks
- 6 oz semi-sweet chocolate, chopped
- 1 tsp vanilla extract
- 1 cup whipped cream (for topping)

Instructions:

1. Preheat oven to 350°F (175°C).
2. In a saucepan, combine milk, cream, sugar, cornstarch, and salt. Cook over medium heat, stirring until thickened.
3. In a separate bowl, whisk egg yolks and temper with some of the hot milk mixture. Gradually add the egg yolks to the saucepan and cook for 2-3 minutes.
4. Remove from heat and stir in chocolate and vanilla extract until smooth.
5. Pour the filling into the prepared pie crust and let cool.
6. Refrigerate for at least 4 hours before serving. Top with whipped cream before serving.

Sweet Potato Pie

Ingredients:

- 2 cups mashed sweet potatoes
- 1/2 cup brown sugar
- 1/2 cup granulated sugar
- 1 tsp cinnamon
- 1/4 tsp nutmeg
- 1/4 tsp ginger
- 1/4 tsp cloves
- 1/2 cup milk
- 2 large eggs, beaten
- 1 tsp vanilla extract
- 1/2 cup melted butter
- 1 prepared pie crust

Instructions:

1. Preheat oven to 350°F (175°C).
2. In a large bowl, combine sweet potatoes, sugars, spices, milk, eggs, vanilla, and butter. Mix well.
3. Pour the mixture into the prepared pie crust.
4. Bake for 45-50 minutes, or until the filling is set.
5. Let cool before serving.

Peach Pie

Ingredients:

- 4 cups fresh peaches, peeled and sliced
- 3/4 cup granulated sugar
- 1/4 cup brown sugar
- 1/4 cup cornstarch
- 1 tbsp lemon juice
- 1/2 tsp cinnamon
- 1/4 tsp nutmeg
- 1 tbsp butter, cut into small pieces
- 1 prepared pie crust

Instructions:

1. Preheat oven to 425°F (220°C).
2. In a large bowl, combine peaches, sugars, cornstarch, lemon juice, cinnamon, and nutmeg. Toss to combine.
3. Roll out one pie crust and place it in a 9-inch pie pan. Pour the peach mixture into the crust and dot with butter.
4. Roll out the second pie crust and place it over the peaches. Trim, seal, and crimp the edges. Cut slits in the top to allow steam to escape.
5. Bake for 45-50 minutes, until the crust is golden and the filling is bubbling.
6. Let cool before serving.

Blackberry Pie

Ingredients:

- 4 cups fresh or frozen blackberries
- 3/4 cup granulated sugar
- 1/4 cup cornstarch
- 1 tbsp lemon juice
- 1 tsp vanilla extract
- 1 tbsp butter
- 1 prepared pie crust

Instructions:

1. Preheat oven to 375°F (190°C).
2. In a saucepan, combine blackberries, sugar, cornstarch, lemon juice, and vanilla extract. Cook over medium heat, stirring until the mixture thickens and starts to boil.
3. Roll out one pie crust and place it in a 9-inch pie pan. Pour the blackberry mixture into the crust and dot with butter.
4. Roll out the second pie crust and place it over the filling. Trim, seal, and crimp the edges. Cut slits in the top for ventilation.
5. Bake for 45-50 minutes, until the crust is golden and the filling is bubbly.
6. Let cool before serving.

Strawberry Rhubarb Pie

Ingredients:

- 2 cups strawberries, hulled and sliced
- 2 cups rhubarb, chopped
- 1 1/2 cups granulated sugar
- 1/4 cup cornstarch
- 1/4 tsp salt
- 1 tbsp lemon juice
- 1 prepared pie crust

Instructions:

1. Preheat oven to 375°F (190°C).
2. In a bowl, combine strawberries, rhubarb, sugar, cornstarch, salt, and lemon juice. Toss to combine.
3. Roll out one pie crust and place it in a 9-inch pie pan. Pour the strawberry-rhubarb mixture into the crust.
4. Roll out the second pie crust and place it over the filling. Trim, seal, and crimp the edges. Cut slits in the top to allow steam to escape.
5. Bake for 45-50 minutes, until the crust is golden and the filling is bubbly.
6. Let cool before serving.

Coconut Cream Pie

Ingredients:

- 1 1/2 cups whole milk
- 1/2 cup heavy cream
- 1/2 cup granulated sugar
- 1/4 cup cornstarch
- 1/4 tsp salt
- 3 large egg yolks, beaten
- 1 1/2 cups sweetened shredded coconut
- 1 tsp vanilla extract
- 1 tbsp butter
- 1 prepared pie crust
- Whipped cream (for topping)

Instructions:

1. Preheat oven to 350°F (175°C).
2. In a saucepan, combine milk, cream, sugar, cornstarch, and salt. Cook over medium heat, stirring until the mixture thickens and starts to boil.
3. In a separate bowl, whisk egg yolks and temper with some of the hot milk mixture. Gradually add the egg yolks to the saucepan and cook for 2-3 minutes.
4. Stir in shredded coconut, vanilla, and butter.
5. Pour the filling into the prepared pie crust.
6. Bake for 20-25 minutes until the filling is set.

7. Let cool, then refrigerate for at least 2 hours before serving. Top with whipped cream before serving.

Custard Pie

Ingredients:

- 1 1/2 cups whole milk
- 1/2 cup heavy cream
- 3 large eggs
- 1/2 cup granulated sugar
- 1 tsp vanilla extract
- 1/4 tsp ground nutmeg
- 1/4 tsp ground cinnamon
- 1 prepared pie crust

Instructions:

1. Preheat oven to 350°F (175°C).
2. In a saucepan, heat milk and cream over medium heat until warm, but not boiling.
3. In a bowl, whisk together eggs, sugar, vanilla, nutmeg, and cinnamon. Gradually whisk in the warm milk mixture.
4. Pour the custard into the prepared pie crust.
5. Bake for 40-45 minutes, until the center is set and the top is golden brown.
6. Let cool before serving.

Lemon Pie

Ingredients:

- 1 1/4 cups granulated sugar
- 1/4 cup cornstarch
- 1 1/2 cups water
- 3 large egg yolks, beaten
- 1/2 cup fresh lemon juice
- 1 tbsp lemon zest
- 2 tbsp butter
- 1 prepared pie crust
- Whipped cream (for topping)

Instructions:

1. Preheat oven to 350°F (175°C).
2. In a saucepan, combine sugar, cornstarch, and water. Cook over medium heat, stirring until the mixture thickens and starts to boil.
3. Gradually whisk in the egg yolks and continue cooking for 2-3 minutes.
4. Stir in lemon juice, lemon zest, and butter.
5. Pour the lemon filling into the prepared pie crust.
6. Bake for 10-12 minutes until set.
7. Let cool before serving. Top with whipped cream before serving.

Mince Pie

Ingredients:

- 1 jar mincemeat (or homemade mincemeat)
- 1/4 cup brandy (optional)
- 1 tbsp lemon juice
- 1 prepared pie crust

Instructions:

1. Preheat oven to 375°F (190°C).
2. In a bowl, combine mincemeat, brandy, and lemon juice.
3. Roll out one pie crust and place it in a 9-inch pie pan. Fill with the mincemeat mixture.
4. Roll out the second pie crust and place it over the filling. Trim, seal, and crimp the edges. Cut slits in the top to allow steam to escape.
5. Bake for 30-35 minutes, until the crust is golden.
6. Let cool before serving.

Maple Cream Pie

Ingredients:

- 1 cup maple syrup
- 1/2 cup heavy cream
- 1/4 cup granulated sugar
- 2 tbsp cornstarch
- 1/2 tsp vanilla extract
- 1 prepared pie crust
- Whipped cream (for topping)

Instructions:

1. Preheat oven to 350°F (175°C).
2. In a saucepan, combine maple syrup, heavy cream, sugar, and cornstarch. Cook over medium heat, stirring until thickened.
3. Stir in vanilla extract.
4. Pour the filling into the prepared pie crust.
5. Bake for 20-25 minutes, until the filling is set.
6. Let cool before serving. Top with whipped cream before serving.

Chocolate Silk Pie

Ingredients:

- 1 1/2 cups semisweet chocolate chips
- 1 cup heavy cream
- 1 tbsp butter
- 3 large eggs
- 1/4 cup granulated sugar
- 1/2 tsp vanilla extract
- 1 prepared graham cracker crust
- Whipped cream (for topping)

Instructions:

1. In a saucepan, melt the chocolate chips with heavy cream and butter over medium heat, stirring until smooth.
2. Remove from heat and whisk in eggs, sugar, and vanilla extract until well combined.
3. Pour the chocolate mixture into the graham cracker crust.
4. Refrigerate for at least 4 hours, or until set.
5. Top with whipped cream before serving.

Raspberry Pie

Ingredients:

- 4 cups fresh raspberries
- 1 1/2 cups granulated sugar
- 1/4 cup cornstarch
- 1 tbsp lemon juice
- 1/4 tsp salt
- 1 prepared pie crust
- 1 tbsp butter, cubed

Instructions:

1. Preheat oven to 375°F (190°C).
2. In a bowl, combine raspberries, sugar, cornstarch, lemon juice, and salt.
3. Pour the filling into the prepared pie crust and dot with butter.
4. Roll out a second pie crust, place it over the pie, and trim, seal, and crimp the edges.
5. Cut slits in the top crust for ventilation.
6. Bake for 45-50 minutes, until the crust is golden and the filling is bubbling.
7. Let cool before serving.

French Silk Pie

Ingredients:

- 1 prepared pie crust
- 8 oz dark chocolate, melted
- 1/4 cup granulated sugar
- 1/4 cup butter, softened
- 2 large eggs
- 1 tsp vanilla extract
- 1 1/2 cups heavy cream, whipped

Instructions:

1. Preheat oven to 350°F (175°C).
2. Bake the prepared pie crust for 10-12 minutes, until golden. Let cool.
3. In a bowl, beat together melted chocolate, sugar, butter, eggs, and vanilla until smooth.
4. Fold in the whipped cream.
5. Pour the filling into the cooled pie crust.
6. Refrigerate for at least 4 hours to set.
7. Top with whipped cream before serving.

Buttermilk Pie

Ingredients:

- 1 prepared pie crust
- 1 1/2 cups granulated sugar
- 1/4 cup all-purpose flour
- 1/2 tsp salt
- 3 large eggs
- 1 1/2 cups buttermilk
- 1/4 cup butter, melted
- 1 tsp vanilla extract

Instructions:

1. Preheat oven to 350°F (175°C).
2. In a mixing bowl, whisk together sugar, flour, salt, eggs, buttermilk, butter, and vanilla.
3. Pour the mixture into the prepared pie crust.
4. Bake for 45-50 minutes, until the filling is set and lightly browned.
5. Let cool before serving.

Meringue Pie

Ingredients:

- 1 prepared pie crust
- 1 1/2 cups granulated sugar
- 1/4 cup cornstarch
- 1 1/2 cups water
- 4 large egg yolks
- 2 tbsp butter
- 1 tsp vanilla extract
- 4 large egg whites
- 1/2 tsp cream of tartar
- 1/4 cup granulated sugar (for meringue)

Instructions:

1. Preheat oven to 350°F (175°C).
2. In a saucepan, combine sugar, cornstarch, and water. Bring to a boil over medium heat, whisking constantly.
3. In a bowl, whisk egg yolks, then slowly add the hot mixture to temper the eggs. Return to heat and cook until thickened.
4. Remove from heat and stir in butter and vanilla. Pour into the prepared pie crust.
5. Beat egg whites with cream of tartar until soft peaks form. Gradually add sugar and continue beating until stiff peaks form.
6. Spread the meringue over the filling, sealing the edges.
7. Bake for 10-15 minutes, until the meringue is golden. Let cool before serving.

Apple Crumble Pie

Ingredients:

- 6 cups peeled and sliced apples (Granny Smith or Honeycrisp)
- 1/2 cup granulated sugar
- 1/2 tsp ground cinnamon
- 1/4 tsp nutmeg
- 1 tbsp lemon juice
- 1/4 cup all-purpose flour
- 1/2 cup rolled oats
- 1/2 cup brown sugar
- 1/4 cup cold butter, cubed
- 1 prepared pie crust

Instructions:

1. Preheat oven to 375°F (190°C).
2. In a bowl, toss the apple slices with sugar, cinnamon, nutmeg, and lemon juice.
3. Pour the apple mixture into the prepared pie crust.
4. In another bowl, mix together flour, oats, brown sugar, and cold butter. Use a pastry cutter to combine until crumbly.
5. Sprinkle the crumble topping over the apples.
6. Bake for 40-45 minutes, until the topping is golden and the filling is bubbling.
7. Let cool before serving.

Caramel Apple Pie

Ingredients:

- 6 cups peeled and sliced apples
- 1/2 cup granulated sugar
- 1/4 cup brown sugar
- 1/4 tsp cinnamon
- 1/4 tsp nutmeg
- 1 tbsp lemon juice
- 1/4 cup cornstarch
- 1/2 cup caramel sauce
- 1 prepared pie crust
- 1 tbsp butter, cubed

Instructions:

1. Preheat oven to 375°F (190°C).
2. In a bowl, toss the apples with sugar, brown sugar, cinnamon, nutmeg, lemon juice, and cornstarch.
3. Pour the apple mixture into the prepared pie crust. Drizzle with caramel sauce and dot with butter.
4. Roll out a second pie crust and place it over the pie. Trim, seal, and crimp the edges.
5. Cut slits in the top crust for ventilation.
6. Bake for 45-50 minutes, until the crust is golden and the filling is bubbling.
7. Let cool before serving.

Mixed Berry Pie

Ingredients:

- 2 cups strawberries, hulled and sliced
- 1 cup blueberries
- 1 cup raspberries
- 1 cup blackberries
- 1 cup granulated sugar
- 2 tbsp cornstarch
- 1 tbsp lemon juice
- 1/4 tsp salt
- 1 prepared pie crust

Instructions:

1. Preheat oven to 375°F (190°C).
2. In a bowl, combine all the berries with sugar, cornstarch, lemon juice, and salt.
3. Pour the berry mixture into the prepared pie crust.
4. Roll out a second pie crust, place it over the pie, and trim, seal, and crimp the edges.
5. Cut slits in the top crust for ventilation.
6. Bake for 40-45 minutes, until the crust is golden and the filling is bubbling.
7. Let cool before serving.

Huckleberry Pie

Ingredients:

- 4 cups fresh huckleberries
- 1 1/4 cups granulated sugar
- 1/4 cup cornstarch
- 1 tbsp lemon juice
- 1/4 tsp salt
- 1 prepared pie crust

Instructions:

1. Preheat oven to 375°F (190°C).
2. In a bowl, mix the huckleberries with sugar, cornstarch, lemon juice, and salt.
3. Pour the filling into the prepared pie crust.
4. Roll out a second pie crust, place it over the pie, and trim, seal, and crimp the edges.
5. Cut slits in the top crust for ventilation.
6. Bake for 45-50 minutes, until the crust is golden and the filling is bubbling.
7. Let cool before serving.

S'mores Pie

Ingredients:

- 1 prepared graham cracker crust
- 1 cup semi-sweet chocolate chips
- 1/2 cup heavy cream
- 2 large eggs
- 1/2 tsp vanilla extract
- 1/2 cup mini marshmallows

Instructions:

1. Preheat oven to 350°F (175°C).
2. In a saucepan, heat heavy cream over medium heat until simmering.
3. Pour the cream over the chocolate chips and stir until smooth.
4. Whisk in eggs and vanilla until well combined.
5. Pour the chocolate mixture into the graham cracker crust.
6. Bake for 20-25 minutes, until the center is set.
7. Top with mini marshmallows and bake for another 2-3 minutes until the marshmallows are toasted.
8. Let cool before serving.

Salted Caramel Pie

Ingredients:

- 1 prepared pie crust
- 1 cup granulated sugar
- 6 tbsp unsalted butter
- 1/2 cup heavy cream
- 1 tsp vanilla extract
- 1/2 tsp sea salt
- 1/4 cup chopped salted pecans (optional)

Instructions:

1. Preheat oven to 350°F (175°C).
2. In a saucepan, heat sugar over medium heat, stirring constantly until it melts and turns amber.
3. Add butter and stir until melted. Gradually add heavy cream and stir until smooth.
4. Remove from heat and stir in vanilla and sea salt.
5. Pour the caramel filling into the prepared pie crust.
6. Refrigerate for at least 2 hours to set.
7. Top with chopped pecans if desired before serving.

Apricot Pie

Ingredients:

- 4 cups fresh apricots, pitted and sliced
- 3/4 cup granulated sugar
- 1/4 cup brown sugar
- 1/4 cup cornstarch
- 1 tbsp lemon juice
- 1/2 tsp cinnamon
- 1 tbsp butter, cut into small pieces
- 1 prepared pie crust

Instructions:

1. Preheat oven to 425°F (220°C).
2. In a large bowl, combine apricots, sugars, cornstarch, lemon juice, and cinnamon. Toss to combine.
3. Roll out one pie crust and place it in a 9-inch pie pan. Pour the apricot mixture into the crust and dot with butter.
4. Roll out the second pie crust and place it over the apricots. Trim, seal, and crimp the edges. Cut slits in the top to allow steam to escape.
5. Bake for 45-50 minutes, until the crust is golden and the filling is bubbling.
6. Let cool before serving.

Pear Pie

Ingredients:

- 5-6 ripe pears, peeled, cored, and sliced
- 3/4 cup granulated sugar
- 1/4 cup brown sugar
- 2 tbsp cornstarch
- 1 tsp ground cinnamon
- 1 tbsp lemon juice
- 1/4 tsp ground nutmeg
- 1 prepared pie crust

Instructions:

1. Preheat oven to 375°F (190°C).
2. In a large bowl, toss the pear slices with sugar, brown sugar, cornstarch, cinnamon, lemon juice, and nutmeg.
3. Roll out one pie crust and place it in a 9-inch pie pan. Pour the pear mixture into the crust.
4. Roll out the second pie crust and place it over the filling. Trim, seal, and crimp the edges. Cut slits in the top for ventilation.
5. Bake for 45-50 minutes, until the crust is golden and the filling is bubbling.
6. Let cool before serving.

Almond Joy Pie

Ingredients:

- 1 1/2 cups shredded coconut
- 1/2 cup chopped almonds
- 1/2 cup semisweet chocolate chips
- 1/4 cup granulated sugar
- 1/4 cup light corn syrup
- 1/4 cup heavy cream
- 1 tsp vanilla extract
- 1 prepared graham cracker crust

Instructions:

1. Preheat oven to 350°F (175°C).
2. In a bowl, combine coconut, almonds, chocolate chips, sugar, corn syrup, heavy cream, and vanilla. Mix until well combined.
3. Pour the filling into the graham cracker crust.
4. Bake for 30-35 minutes, until the filling is set and golden brown on top.
5. Let cool before serving.

Honey Pie

Ingredients:

- 1 cup honey
- 1/2 cup heavy cream
- 3 large eggs
- 1/4 cup granulated sugar
- 1 tbsp cornstarch
- 1/2 tsp vanilla extract
- 1/4 tsp ground cinnamon
- 1 prepared pie crust

Instructions:

1. Preheat oven to 350°F (175°C).
2. In a saucepan, combine honey and heavy cream. Heat over medium heat until warm.
3. In a bowl, whisk eggs, sugar, cornstarch, vanilla extract, and cinnamon. Gradually add the warm honey mixture, whisking constantly.
4. Pour the filling into the prepared pie crust.
5. Bake for 35-40 minutes, until the filling is set and slightly golden on top.
6. Let cool before serving.

Brown Sugar Pie

Ingredients:

- 1 1/2 cups brown sugar
- 1/2 cup heavy cream
- 1/4 cup unsalted butter, melted
- 2 large eggs
- 1 tsp vanilla extract
- 1 tbsp cornstarch
- 1 prepared pie crust

Instructions:

1. Preheat oven to 350°F (175°C).
2. In a bowl, whisk together brown sugar, heavy cream, melted butter, eggs, vanilla, and cornstarch.
3. Pour the filling into the prepared pie crust.
4. Bake for 40-45 minutes, until the filling is set and golden brown on top.
5. Let cool before serving.

Orange Cream Pie

Ingredients:

- 1 1/2 cups fresh orange juice
- 1 tbsp grated orange zest
- 1/2 cup granulated sugar
- 2 tbsp cornstarch
- 1/4 tsp salt
- 3 large egg yolks, beaten
- 1 cup heavy cream
- 1 prepared pie crust

Instructions:

1. Preheat oven to 350°F (175°C).
2. In a saucepan, combine orange juice, orange zest, sugar, cornstarch, and salt. Heat over medium heat, stirring until the mixture thickens and begins to boil.
3. Gradually whisk in the egg yolks and continue cooking for 2-3 minutes.
4. Stir in heavy cream and cook for another 2-3 minutes.
5. Pour the filling into the prepared pie crust.
6. Bake for 20-25 minutes, until the filling is set.
7. Let cool before serving.

Kiwi Pie

Ingredients:

- 6-8 ripe kiwis, peeled and sliced
- 1/2 cup granulated sugar
- 1/4 cup cornstarch
- 1/2 tsp vanilla extract
- 1 tbsp lime juice
- 1 prepared pie crust

Instructions:

1. Preheat oven to 350°F (175°C).
2. In a bowl, mix together sugar, cornstarch, vanilla extract, and lime juice.
3. Fold in the kiwi slices and toss to coat evenly.
4. Pour the kiwi mixture into the prepared pie crust.
5. Bake for 25-30 minutes, until the filling is set and the crust is golden.
6. Let cool before serving.

Peanut Butter Pie

Ingredients:

- 1 cup peanut butter
- 1 cup powdered sugar
- 1/2 cup heavy cream
- 1 tsp vanilla extract
- 1 prepared graham cracker crust

Instructions:

1. In a bowl, mix peanut butter, powdered sugar, heavy cream, and vanilla until smooth.
2. Pour the peanut butter mixture into the graham cracker crust.
3. Refrigerate for at least 3 hours, or until set.
4. Top with whipped cream before serving.

Ice Cream Pie

Ingredients:

- 1 1/2 cups crushed graham crackers
- 1/4 cup granulated sugar
- 1/4 cup unsalted butter, melted
- 3 cups your favorite ice cream, softened
- 1/2 cup hot fudge sauce (optional)
- Whipped cream (for topping)

Instructions:

1. Preheat oven to 350°F (175°C).
2. In a bowl, combine crushed graham crackers, sugar, and melted butter. Press the mixture into a 9-inch pie pan.
3. Bake for 8-10 minutes until golden brown. Let cool completely.
4. Once the crust is cooled, fill with softened ice cream. Smooth the top.
5. Freeze for at least 4 hours, or until firm.
6. Top with hot fudge sauce and whipped cream before serving.

Chiffon Pie

Ingredients:

- 1/2 cup orange juice
- 1 tbsp unflavored gelatin
- 1/2 cup granulated sugar
- 3 large egg yolks
- 1 tbsp lemon juice
- 1/2 cup whipped cream
- 1 prepared graham cracker crust

Instructions:

1. In a small bowl, sprinkle the gelatin over the orange juice and let it bloom for about 5 minutes.
2. In a saucepan, heat the sugar, egg yolks, and lemon juice over medium heat, whisking constantly until the mixture thickens.
3. Remove from heat, add the gelatin mixture, and stir until dissolved.
4. Let the mixture cool to room temperature.
5. Once cooled, fold in the whipped cream until well combined.
6. Pour the filling into the prepared graham cracker crust.
7. Refrigerate for at least 3 hours, or until set.
8. Serve with additional whipped cream on top.

Rhubarb Pie

Ingredients:

- 4 cups fresh rhubarb, chopped
- 1 1/4 cups granulated sugar
- 2 tbsp cornstarch
- 1 tbsp lemon juice
- 1/4 tsp salt
- 1 prepared pie crust

Instructions:

1. Preheat oven to 400°F (200°C).
2. In a large bowl, combine rhubarb, sugar, cornstarch, lemon juice, and salt. Toss to coat.
3. Pour the rhubarb mixture into the prepared pie crust.
4. Roll out the second pie crust and place it over the rhubarb filling. Trim, seal, and crimp the edges. Cut slits in the top to allow steam to escape.
5. Bake for 45-50 minutes, until the crust is golden and the filling is bubbling.
6. Let cool before serving.

Pineapple Pie

Ingredients:

- 1 can (20 oz) crushed pineapple, drained
- 1 cup granulated sugar
- 1/4 cup cornstarch
- 1/4 tsp salt
- 3 large eggs, beaten
- 1 tbsp butter, melted
- 1/2 tsp vanilla extract
- 1 prepared pie crust

Instructions:

1. Preheat oven to 350°F (175°C).
2. In a saucepan, combine pineapple, sugar, cornstarch, and salt. Cook over medium heat, stirring constantly, until the mixture thickens.
3. Remove from heat and stir in the beaten eggs, butter, and vanilla.
4. Pour the mixture into the prepared pie crust.
5. Bake for 30-35 minutes, until the filling is set and the crust is golden.
6. Let cool before serving.

Mocha Pie

Ingredients:

- 1 1/2 cups heavy cream
- 1/2 cup strong brewed coffee, cooled
- 1/4 cup granulated sugar
- 8 oz semi-sweet chocolate, chopped
- 1 tsp vanilla extract
- 1 prepared chocolate cookie crust

Instructions:

1. In a saucepan, combine heavy cream, coffee, and sugar. Heat over medium heat, stirring occasionally, until the sugar dissolves.
2. Remove from heat and stir in the chopped chocolate until melted and smooth.
3. Stir in the vanilla extract.
4. Pour the mixture into the prepared chocolate cookie crust.
5. Refrigerate for at least 4 hours, or until the pie is set.
6. Serve with whipped cream and chocolate shavings on top.

Blackberry Custard Pie

Ingredients:

- 2 cups fresh blackberries
- 3/4 cup granulated sugar
- 1 tbsp cornstarch
- 1/2 cup heavy cream
- 3 large eggs
- 1 tsp vanilla extract
- 1/4 tsp salt
- 1 prepared pie crust

Instructions:

1. Preheat oven to 375°F (190°C).
2. In a bowl, combine blackberries, sugar, and cornstarch. Toss to coat.
3. In a separate bowl, whisk together heavy cream, eggs, vanilla, and salt.
4. Pour the cream mixture over the blackberries in the pie crust.
5. Bake for 40-45 minutes, until the custard is set and the crust is golden.
6. Let cool before serving.

Chocolate Peanut Butter Pie

Ingredients:

- 1 prepared graham cracker crust
- 1 cup creamy peanut butter
- 1 cup powdered sugar
- 1/2 cup heavy cream
- 4 oz semi-sweet chocolate, chopped
- 1 tbsp butter

Instructions:

1. In a bowl, mix peanut butter and powdered sugar until smooth.
2. Add the heavy cream and mix until the mixture is fluffy.
3. Spread the peanut butter mixture into the prepared pie crust.
4. In a saucepan, melt the chocolate and butter over low heat, stirring constantly until smooth.
5. Pour the melted chocolate over the peanut butter filling.
6. Refrigerate for at least 4 hours, or until set.
7. Serve with whipped cream and chopped peanuts on top.

Praline Pie

Ingredients:

- 1 prepared pie crust
- 1 cup light brown sugar
- 1/2 cup heavy cream
- 1/2 cup chopped pecans
- 1/4 cup butter, melted
- 2 large eggs
- 1 tsp vanilla extract
- 1/4 tsp salt

Instructions:

1. Preheat oven to 350°F (175°C).
2. In a mixing bowl, whisk together brown sugar, heavy cream, butter, eggs, vanilla, and salt.
3. Stir in the chopped pecans until well combined.
4. Pour the mixture into the prepared pie crust.
5. Bake for 45-50 minutes, until the pie is set and golden.
6. Let cool before serving.

Banana Foster Pie

Ingredients:

- 1 prepared graham cracker crust
- 2 ripe bananas, sliced
- 1/2 cup brown sugar
- 2 tbsp butter
- 2 tbsp dark rum
- 1/4 tsp cinnamon
- 1/4 tsp vanilla extract
- 1 cup heavy cream, whipped

Instructions:

1. In a saucepan, melt butter and brown sugar over medium heat. Stir until smooth.
2. Add the sliced bananas, cinnamon, and vanilla, and cook for 2-3 minutes.
3. Stir in the rum and cook for an additional 1 minute, then remove from heat.
4. Pour the banana mixture into the prepared graham cracker crust.
5. Top with whipped cream and refrigerate for at least 2 hours.
6. Serve chilled.

Bourbon Pecan Pie

Ingredients:

- 1 prepared pie crust
- 1 1/2 cups pecan halves
- 1/2 cup corn syrup
- 1/2 cup granulated sugar
- 1/4 cup bourbon
- 3 large eggs
- 1/4 tsp salt
- 1 tsp vanilla extract
- 1 tbsp melted butter

Instructions:

1. Preheat oven to 350°F (175°C).
2. In a large bowl, whisk together corn syrup, sugar, bourbon, eggs, salt, and vanilla.
3. Stir in melted butter and pecans.
4. Pour the mixture into the prepared pie crust.
5. Bake for 50-55 minutes, until the filling is set and the crust is golden.
6. Let cool before serving.

Bourbon Sweet Potato Pie

Ingredients:

- 2 cups cooked and mashed sweet potatoes
- 1/2 cup granulated sugar
- 1/2 cup brown sugar
- 1/2 cup heavy cream
- 1/4 cup bourbon
- 2 large eggs
- 1/2 tsp cinnamon
- 1/4 tsp nutmeg
- 1/4 tsp ginger
- 1 prepared pie crust

Instructions:

1. Preheat oven to 350°F (175°C).
2. In a bowl, combine mashed sweet potatoes, granulated sugar, brown sugar, heavy cream, bourbon, eggs, and spices.
3. Mix until smooth and well combined.
4. Pour the mixture into the prepared pie crust.
5. Bake for 45-50 minutes, until the filling is set and the crust is golden.
6. Let cool before serving.

Grapefruit Pie

Ingredients:

- 1 prepared pie crust
- 1 cup freshly squeezed grapefruit juice
- 1/2 cup granulated sugar
- 3 large eggs
- 1/4 cup cornstarch
- 1/2 cup water
- 1 tsp lemon juice
- 1/4 tsp salt
- 1 tbsp butter, cubed

Instructions:

1. Preheat oven to 350°F (175°C).
2. In a saucepan, combine grapefruit juice, sugar, cornstarch, water, lemon juice, and salt.
3. Cook over medium heat, stirring constantly, until the mixture thickens.
4. In a bowl, whisk the eggs and slowly add the hot mixture to temper the eggs.
5. Pour the egg mixture back into the saucepan and cook for another 2 minutes.
6. Remove from heat and stir in butter.
7. Pour the filling into the prepared pie crust.
8. Bake for 30-35 minutes, until the filling is set.
9. Let cool before serving.

Spiced Pear Pie

Ingredients:

- 4 ripe pears, peeled, cored, and sliced
- 1/2 cup granulated sugar
- 1/4 cup brown sugar
- 1/4 tsp cinnamon
- 1/4 tsp nutmeg
- 1/4 tsp allspice
- 1 tbsp lemon juice
- 2 tbsp cornstarch
- 1 prepared pie crust

Instructions:

1. Preheat oven to 375°F (190°C).
2. In a large bowl, toss the pear slices with sugar, brown sugar, cinnamon, nutmeg, allspice, lemon juice, and cornstarch.
3. Pour the pear mixture into the prepared pie crust.
4. Roll out the second pie crust and place it over the filling. Trim, seal, and crimp the edges. Cut slits in the top crust.
5. Bake for 45-50 minutes, until the crust is golden and the filling is bubbling.
6. Let cool before serving.

www.ingramcontent.com/pod-product-compliance
Lightning Source LLC
LaVergne TN
LVHW081322060526
838201LV00055B/2410